Loose Cannon

Sierra-Nicole Qualles

TABLE OF CONTENTS

Up Side

Whole Identity
is (

)

Speaking in Ribbits

more of the following
marked on stages: recovery version
shutdowns are in season and thumbs pointing west
waiting for the look beyond

remember when everyone was to blame
headlines half the story and half a price
an easy to use country

now credits fly
over pigs that eat steak
and a people who hop
into abduction

If It Came to That

jammed into the other choice
he knows an opening

a new breath
            a cost of chaos under the moon

there is a devotion
the longing to not let go

even as paradise screams, *stop*

The Osiris Key Party

nuclear heart ticking help
it was the spring sight that doomed us
before we could move, our bodies eviscerated
into our own maddening ideas

pushing our final thoughts to
completion
we choose the right fleshy keys
the weathered tenses are confused again

The Victory of D.B. Cooper

I step off into stillness
the outlined fall
and further air
bridging with bills
between freedom and cuffs
and it is I
who triggers fate
and lets go
from the echoed plane
from stars
into what is unsolved
not on earth
but in headlines
out of reach
in rain

They Don't Know Where They Are

You think it's
groovy
to mix bee stings
and water
stalling out life
for the more dynamic
good riddance
while understanding
little and always moving
always

A Badly Timed Phenomenon

a comet carried
trapped, rocking a Toyota
put the window down to see the white flag waving
the world surrendering to a back seat

tail spreads dust on the road
making what is behind complete

a security of nothing
a sudden urge to look up
the comet's envelope waiting to be filled by the sun

while few stay for this stray
while some run from the road
while others press their eyes to coffee cups
face down, backs to the sky

sometimes there's more to pay attention to than space
Sometimes there's nothing at all

Spilled Empires Require Only That You Hate

Only inhaling moisture from your paws
can save what is left of evening
This distance holds onto the sick requirements of breathing

(Had I run into America sooner,
            I would have lost lines of backskin)

I love your idea of death in '94
            and how I resemble revolutions

Your hand with its rifle prayed once

-*We are starting this life*-

between bear traps and plantations looking to restock

I know we've misplaced ourselves on the trail
            and that the absence of color is before us
The sudden resistance we were caught with –
but hold

You dug too many graves the day I lost my balance

Stead of Kisses

Torn note and the mark
A frantic reach for the bed
And here it is, the fear
The sick
The laughter,
The sounds of the end of time

And the postponed pulse
Vacationing from the afterlife
Laces addiction and curse
And says, “shut up,” to feel it

Yet it isn’t led to the sheets
It is buried there
Between temper and temperature
While the carcass prints
Swallow the ungathered night

Gray Couch

for Mom

spider crawl snake eyes
ninja beloved by the straight path
by the stairs leading to dark
through the walls under marble sky
squeezed up to target contentment

mission accomplished
champion of the repeat pattern
and none the wiser
settled into cold gray

Legend's Blues

Only monsters wake up early
The queen dances behind the king
The troops march toward a closed eternity
May never came but the air did
Waving and hanging its stock over
Crouching whispers

Is it winter yet

The open eye holds tension
Is this game a new genius or the last
Isis feathers the way
But the labor is Eileithyia's

It is a disposable game
A deplorable stampede
Toiled
And clothed
In the expectations of an experiment
Oh days that fall on empty men

Big Mac and Uncle Tom Take Five

Time out
This line is long for Brogan feet
And I keep taking five
Although the commercials
Beckon blackness through golden arches
The chorus of
“Yes sir, no sir, yes sir, yessir, yessir, nosir, nahsir, nahsir, number five sir, yes sir, take five sir”
Could make even the Dead
Hear that whip cracking to the beat

There were appearing cuts on my
hands
While I ordered blood in my
supersized shoes
Little Eva on her deathbed
Promised Heaven
If we just put the shackles down

Ray Kroc on his deathbed
Promised Heaven
If we just ordered that shake

But that Sax never said

On its deathbed

bada bop ba ba
And there is no freedom
When you’re knee deep in dollar menus
I learned this when Simon Legree
Told me how he’s lovin’ it.
And how it’s
teaching us our place

Jugular's Atlas

withered out doorsteps
a surprise attack
is getting closer

[She breathes in glass intervals]

will everything be ok after piercing?
after creased perception dwindles?

the smile ready for disintegration
stands rocking on the bookshelf
there is an off chance the ink is still wet

Reacting to Shadows

It is revealed, the nature of beings in hell
Waiting by books filled with mutterings and
Ripped skin. Wednesday
I misplaced my strength. Saturday
My soul dead. Today
I am crushed by lightness
Below Edgar and Ezra
Not talking, drinking
After drinking, jumping
No tenderness in sandless unconscious

A spell cast, is it 90th or GO th

Is it poetry or truth drowning in the kingdom of the sea
Is it me or Annabelle Lee
Or is it the moon's fire
That is choking

It's all desire
And 26 damn letters
Can't change
The edge and easy

Suspended Dreaming of Little Boots

I Caligula (who will never be mine)
Escaped with me
On the tightrope
With no concern in his eyes

II The dare was the voyage
His laurel wreath
Started piercing his scalp
As he giggled, trampling

III Tomorrow he will want it all
But now he will settle
With his fireside chats
With the moon

IV But I wondered when we
Would be seized and shaken
Out of our spirits
Out of our "Hails"

V And I wonder when he
Will say that I too
Am Caesar
And that my ghost, like his
Is trapped under my sole

Str_nger

trying
not so gracefully
                                                            into the sphere

the ought and considerable
desirable   leery
chanced mistakes
   paused   wants
who are you,
            sinking
I've broken eyes
(repaired twitches)

come now while you can see
it has been found
yes
It has been found,
yes?

don't move

silence knows you're coming
and it is sorry to be without vibrations

Acqu___tance

biased eyes
you shout need to shadow

are you here?

morning curtain
I've postponed it long enough,
you can break now, again
fully
tidal

don't worry it'll happen
and it is on your side

I've heard enough of truth
found you in forks
            but
It's never ruin

Fri_nd

here in hot is it
C hello
clock o 9 my, bad my
funeral a to pajamas wearing you are why?
cement the up screaming you saw I
bastard jellyfish you, loneliness hi

better all we.
be better

coke diet now?
happy you are, day one dead be to going I'm
indulge, indulge pencil America of Bank
run, words hated
rum run words treated
order
odor low, Expo, it do can you
room this from, rum, rum, run, run

Ene_y

run, run, rum, rum, from this room
you can do it, Expo, low odor
order
treated words run rum
hated words, run
Bank of America pencil, indulge, indulge
I'm going to be dead one day, are you happy
now diet coke?

better be
we all better.

hi loneliness, you jellyfish bastard
I saw you screaming up the cement
why are you wearing pajamas to a funeral?
my bad, my 9 o clock
hello C
it is hot in here

Not Guilty

injustice and slices of bread
phenomena of the human condition

amenities are at the end of a pen
pick through the trash
              risks of the not guilty

Pursuit Remembered

Minutes from existence
Forgiveness spears itself two ways
Into the forgetful wilderness
Can it be believed?
What is good and true can be left in a special hurry
What is lost is shaken out of glory
And the paths footless
Can be erased in a rage as haunting as an untouched door
But this is more or less true
To finish anything is

To Pay the Price of Being Hell Bound

40s and Hail Marys
streets looking for an outlet
some kind of exit out of expectations covered in sirens

a beat consistent in aggression
a man seen for who he is
an existence flashed out of rhymes
played over and over in shadows ready to die

who has lived the life knows the rules
who carries “thug” on skin or soul
holds a mirror to the world
who is wild and counts down the years of his life is loved by God

Explaining Poetry to a Dead Rabbit

Destiny is negative
All manners of circles come pulsing
It's not noisy
But to read it backward is sacrifice
It is like forgetting how you died
how that eagle snapped your neck
and called its children up for breakfast
It is me by your side
shoe to head nudging
Saying sorry only to the blood and waking up

How tiring it is when you are your only fear
When the cost of letters
segregates the opened mind

To see the blades of grass as you do
For you to know what it feels like to be safe

The separation of skin and bone has widened
for the words

That endless highway keeping me up
that last touch of dirt crawling in your ear
and the creek from here to sky
motioning complete

Three Tongues Tied

I'd speak the edge of you
Вечно
Letting go of this line
Breaking down in conversion

Was ist jetzt?
Why are you left in the mirror?
Between или and oder
And the expectations of changing

I hear a way through this
Out of the rolling
Пожалуйста
Out of the scrapping
Bitte

Я не понимаю Ja
Ich verstehe Я
The key is forsaking

Centralia, Pennsylvania

The city said
"I'm in love with you,
Run"

you make me think of handcuffs
Maybe I can do more damage

Maybe
There is gasoline in your hair.

Stop. outweigh your life

Call it
invasion of suffocation

Do you snap your ankles to the sound of fire?

best thing to do:
wallow in it
mutual desperation
raggedy

I broke my heart while playing with carbon monoxide

-If nothing else
Light the if-

the road is stained with
inconvenience

and

I hear defiance crackling inside

Believe In

sleeping nova
I've thought of a name
hid it in
speed bumped
kiwi pills

parasitic girls in tunnels
speak to me the
silver rad costs
that would
level me in junk

eat a saga
liars called me Crown
and
I brought the birth to your doorstep

and asked you
for peace this once
while
you bit off my fingernails

Confession and Slow-motion Catastrophe

body parts and half a ghost
dismissed thumping

this is the right way to let someone down
personal lives are ruining the sunset and
the ridden mountains
swallow thought

Leader's Last

wind promised more bad news
the ripping of the dark catches
the back of the skull
and time passes like every letter
burning.

All that's ripped in shadow
in rain
in remembering the saying
"Hello" to the never ending day

All doors pass me in the night
All reflections cry out a tongueless
Halt
All creation has come to see me

To smother in no more
To chant and mark the fate
of a chill and shiver, in the first heaviness
of an awakening eye
and maybe this time if I don't check
and maybe this time if I don't move
out of a bloodless position of birth
I can crawl under the embraces
of the captured

It can be untold
I've heard that the will to live
can be unraveled

Approaching permanence

5150

she looks like a woman who's been chased
a pasted swear and an etched negotiator
between chained elevens
living in the old future
forgetting the color of gravity
while choosing to stay in stains

Say her slanted pleas
Say her changed style
the left side of life
and what it does to the same kind of monsters

as she, as the stolen storm
as the scalpel breaded with advertisements
ready to help if she only signs
her name in the ventilated hallelujah

and the buzzing nature of readiness
keeps her records filed
in the congested hopes
in all the lectures that have been clotted

against that tightness she feels
letting the idea of an exhale go

A Barred Loop

recreation of an identity
who you were smothered under orange and steel
uncovering a situation
                    as transparent as bait
and broken clocks of flesh

have you been inside?

          have you been through the young?
have you been above the unwilling?

behind the eyes lie filth

the skull
                    the pelvis

the action and the watch and again
you dream by schoolyards?

Pre-Instructions

Keep it shut, away
from body and
ink. Wait!
Mail the letter
ripped and make
sure there are enough
bullets
for the rain.

Instructions

Remember if our
words must die
Let them go the way of Распутин
Let them experience every kind of end.

Post-Instructions

Never watch them:
the flexures of legend
the trumpeters of MORE.
They forget,
regularly,
how history is spelled
and every movement is
unforgivable.

Bridge of Trees

I see you on the bridge of trees smiling   with no
enthusiasm with
curled fingers and a sweater a size too big
over shoulders waving goodbye   or hello
or
waving a motion nonexistent for the living
only you could see and I felt myself dying not   into
death not into
life but away far away in place
where your mind met the cement and you know no words
I write can redo March or any time before that now mantled and
shooing me into a reckless
present
replaying a guilt replaying
a hatred for gravity that couldn't just once keep you up
maybe seasons will change but not in this mind

Acidic Crossing

So where is the priest
            who forms toy animals out of
heartbeats mangled
stomachs lined of money
and practiced graves?

Sorted victims and villains
are what ripple spheres
all between tongues
and humiliation

Unless midnight rock
in recollection
repeats the process of throwing up
in the womb, don't be too full
of rage to complete a sentence

Instead, when you can't stand
the thought of a name
and the concept of a road outside your door
rashes the back of your eyes

take special care on how you let go
of silence
and how ascension remains illegal

The Classified

Leading the charge with profane thoughts, saying:
"　　it's here in the whispered shell,
"　　the pulling of what needs to be
"　　the needs of none and all
"　　of one revenge against revenge
"　　of a crossing peace be with
"　　alphabet over alphabet
"　　the running of ideals over G
"　　and Greed over I
"　　and all of us waiting for the next:
"　　*you're it* to be determined

To answer

I am nowhere
Playing backwards
With my eyes in fields

It comes down between
The lot of collided cars
And the dog under the cliff

It is enough to only know a place at night
As long as you are the diving bird

The Feathers of Devils

Named over echoes of mountains, I'm told all bodies decay
in wilderness, in grey furred memories of Moe running into wood and
spinning to saints while being young and bearded

I smell of artifacts, a physical history and hide in closets
painting prayers into "where-are-you" chants
Darkness starts, light manipulates and edges define a pelvis cut
A dying years ago with facts forgotten

This surname that trails me means to die in a nonexistent place
There is no movement but this
No healing in the blindfolded day

Those who can find me follow the feathers of devils
Those who know me know that they might well be mine
But I have promises to keep and forget often where footprints come
from
In the echoes of mountains someone will be found running from decay

Repeat

Anger son
Hold ransom the desire,
                                        The trailing, the whispering
Lift flight, uncover plague, prepare revenge
Linger,
            Battle,
                        Prevail and perish dishonor
Forever eyes fondling heaven
Away, Achilles,
Free (Alone)
                        To bondage destiny

Never Dead   Never the Same

For C

ride through lights a world with emphasis
how prayers can't be said without you
down streets stretching around futures without names

moments see that we are worth it
  yet we are not devoted to days

a duo of sleepless weapons

Tupac and a continuous hunt for pain killers
enough to handle in minds that are always lost

hope between the heat and freezing
hope, a casualty of our language

what do you call this safety?
what do you feel on your way up in the mirrored elevator?

strangers see us in the city after midnight
    where on earth we call home

Petting Hope

Hidden in the blinds with
scratchy Basquiat covers
in the foreground
I saw the practiced, faceless
and traced them with my spoon

I won't eat you soon Anubis
but I won't be fresh either
and on top of the canvassed explanation
I promised
I'd season in all
the sexual Decembers you needed

But if you pleaded to
wrap me in
ideas you thought were good
remember that sometimes
I am allergic to reason
and your existence
is only a good idea in the shade

Clyde's Bonnie

she rises open
banks in harmony condense this darkness
unseen while running
in fragments framing lucid sounds

can she forgive a created quiet?
she claims a neck imprinted in her hands
mine perhaps
mine only

Last Pitch for Consciousness

dig
the wolf is still home

dig
the sea is still growing

dig
the light is still frightened

dig
the ghost is still sorry

dig
the ghost is still sorry

dig
the ghost is still sorry

Of His Birth

out of millennium into standby
        the richness of noise
it is the old man carrying water
the broken waltz

all places have been corrected

guilt, the great instrument of time
is unwelcomed out of cage
the heart beats the shield, the mind
and the hand hides in the skin of voices

what is corrected is unhealthy
        but what of mistakes
has craving always been an illusion
can a question mark give up

this is a calculation, bad love
and full of form

        there in the plastic hour
        are the cries of forgiveness
reconciled, placed inside fever

The Wiener Riesenrad Reunion

I didn't come to turn
But to understand
Yet I am turning between
Your smiles and threats
And you are more concerned
With tablets than my quest for facts
And Anna who only exists to you
In fog or at the end
Of your fingertips wishes you
Dead and safe
Again
And nobody thinks in terms of human beings?
Certainly not you
You left your conscience in your grave
Or in the sewers
Or maybe right there where you
Imagine I'll fall after you shoot me
Me, the most unwise
Providing the cuckoo clock
And you, leaving me little choice
Except to watch you escape
Again

Tontine

jolty engine laughs
and
half a spider chair

recycled shit

the screen light went missing
while I've been here

alive

finally waiting for the
fight outside, knocking

bodies transform into trains
you were "sometimes"

key scissors
I see the chapel that was

incomplete minds, pregnant money

are you tired of death being our song

The Roof of the Knickerbocker Hotel

Rosabelle, believe
believe in the replace
the mirrors
and the clearest zero

zero, both act and freedom
I, both artist and doubt
and you with the key
in your cheek

between tears and séances
chains give me pause
my ruptured escape has
captured me

suspended and submerged
did you really expect me
for ten years to say “Believe”
and did I let you down

when the lights came on and showed
it wasn’t a trick but a bow

Left Winged

Right Winged

It's so low
It's solo

High enough
to choke concentration
Tinkering tinkering in
cracked page turns

Screaming screaming in
inked oral flows

I've switched to red frames
and blue brains

Hatred behind the skin
will go unpublished
Despair will become
famous

Spoken Ted

I kid
I'm Control
Sometimes tranquil feel
My minutes hours
Fruitfully possible
Essence, calm
In part I'm you

True

No tragedy situation
I, wonderful dedicated loving
We focus lives
We attended gamble
No abuse saying, "Leave"
Solid hope, honestly

Pornography

Young sideways
People – garbage
Across harder graphic
I this
I'm violence
I'm blaming

Crystallizing

Dealing inhibitions
Wrong was wrong
I know God
I hope grief
I deserve society

It's Your Way of Talk, We Can Be Where We Will

Where is viridian
Did it go from these hands
Blinded and dipped in the color J?

No I's anymore

For___, the scavenge
The bloody blink of the world
And the verse

___ must look better
Since washing the scent
___ must remember to feed the graves

There will be more under the grass
Between known
And good

Chants can be jammed
But only under a flag on a cool day

Routine

Astute and silent
More waiting under the bridge than known
That endless tune in cables suspended
Creation vibrating
            the figures breath through the bridge

a wave of looking down
secrets pack the foundation and

an interlude of mudcrawls takes
what's left of the light

this bridge will be out of order tomorrow
for more rest than repair

To ask forever

For Jasmine

My hands are the grease of caves
There is rarely time left
To spare you a sign

You'll see my echo in
You'll find me hunting by
And know, and now, and then

More Cage

bumping into light
rebellion contracted the on/off hour
only and forever will hope be
ready for the rape of the altitudes
the stench of chariots in the sky
a hairless wretch rolling in an unmapped stare

it's no problem getting money out of sins
no issue to replace a fold

tonight expect a raid
another hope
another parade
and all will spill their knees
onto a more realistic refusal
begging and splitting their claws
into action

the awakening of blood
will be half EZ
half World War

leaning may come to be the failing of man

while the resurrected stay broken
while the resurrected stay

Ferocious Dots

taking precautions to pick up time
teeth grown out of trees find white splattered throughout grass
soft sight of the wretched, a yelping covered in ants
a rock unknotting moss the true future
a casket under a bridge of wolf fur
today leaving regret inside tomorrow
a cold signature
red lightness coming
a bastard dear old friend
a message in the answer in a lie
turn over
the scars of a flying lesson
violins awakening in brutality
who have I owned without you?
seen running past the bush with a head of a broken radio
seen ribbons over cobblestone over blood
the truth never loved never capable
dirt inching in the insides of nerves
bones painted with fingerprints
no more room for a collection
one engine a hundred wheels
and a doubt we'll make it on time
to the parade and wake
a dishonored lateness
hair edging over
a guillotine the appropriate window
hellos always heard in the back of things
a girl taking pictures of what she does not know
belonging to nothing
a belonging to a guided nothing
the desire to dance
a whispering declaration of war
before breakfast before the thunder gets here
remember the clarity of the lock
remember the dogs marching
the moon bruised at midnight
I'm opening now the lost city
with scissors and curiosity

lust at the end of hooks
a dear friend a bastard
whose language is blacked out
an experiment with the mail
buzzed out messages saying, "come home"
this need for eight eyes and a web
"a pleasant sight" the papers say
"no need for more holes in the wall"
oh my, I'm coming home
earplugs and a pack of glue
tools that make a president smile
lines that make a moose tired
napping on the basketball courts
cheers for a talking section
and the front lines damning
chasm and a distortion of sheets
an ancient human checking the electric bill
hunger for drawings in flames
a deep institution
this continent of whiskers
thumbs extended west
gods swimming home in the sea
a return to cleanliness
how did any of us know that gold was the answer?
you with my favorite hands
an angel waiting to live
kneel with me the guillotine waits
continued moaning a receipt Madame for the morning
too many theys to be completed
naturally there is no interaction
a spring man a fall man
a between hush of extremes
this livelihood with nothing together
harmonica knell the rock cracked
ants taking an inhale of the sunrise
while justified fathers promise the apocalypse for $2.50
these streets are real just above the only detail that is
knives a curious tool for love
the paint needs shedding
glass colors of mistakes
"you'll never be inside me again," says the paper
no need for more holes in the wall
july's shooting star, bad timing

this matter of extinction
the difference between a zero an o and a neighbor's yawn
no immunity
a silliness sold at the booth
tickets for eight please
for all eyes for clarity
a lock of flies
guts counterclockwise
rights stripped in a rhyming scheme
trees bitching and moanin'
congress is in session
a timetable in excess
with the coffee pot half baked
why yes I've seen the wolf's speech at dawn
why yes beauty died on leap year
the funeral was held on a bush
sounds of a flood and purr
left here in the dishes
words undo a wretchedness
a feeling returns unguided
nothing unraveling in moss

www.ingramcontent.com/pod-product-compliance
Lightning Source LLC
Chambersburg PA
CBHW030458010526
44118CB00011B/998
* 9 7 8 0 9 9 9 2 1 0 3 6 9 *